PARAKEET FARMING FOR BEGINNER

A Complete Guide To Raising, Breeding, And Caring For Healthy Budgies   With Expert Tips On Nutrition, Housing, And Training

Holden bodhi

ontents

DISCLAIMER

The information provided in this book, is intended for educational and informational purposes only. The content is based on research, personal experiences, and general knowledge about farming. It is not intended to substitute professional advice or expert consultation. Readers are encouraged to seek professional guidance when implementing any practices or techniques discussed in this book.

The author and publisher make no representations or warranties of any kind regarding the accuracy, applicability, or completeness of the contents of this book. Any reliance you place on such information is strictly at your own risk. The author and publisher shall not be held liable for any damages, losses, or injuries resulting from the use of the information provided.

Additionally, the author does not endorse, recommend, or affiliate with any individual, product, service, website, organization, or brand mentioned or referenced in this book. Any such references are solely for informational purposes, and no warranty or guarantee is implied. The inclusion of these references does not imply any endorsement or partnership by the author.

By reading this book, you acknowledge and accept that the author and publisher are not responsible for any consequences arising from your use of the information provided.

CHAPTER ONE

Overview Of Parakeet Agriculture

For anybody interested in trying out a new pastime or business opportunity, as well as bird aficionados, parakeet farming may be a fulfilling and delightful endeavor. These little, vibrant birds are perfect for farming because of their amiable disposition and endearing habits. This tutorial will assist you in navigating the key components of parakeet farming, whether your goal is to raise parakeets as pets, breed them for the market, or just learn more about their upkeep.

This chapter will cover the fundamentals of raising parakeets, from recognizing their behavior to creating the ideal habitat for their success. We'll talk about the advantages of keeping parakeets, such as their widespread appeal as companion animals and their comparatively minimal care requirements in contrast to other livestock kinds. Furthermore, we will explore the most regularly cultivated parakeet breeds and provide a synopsis of their traits to assist you in choosing the ideal breed for your farming objectives.

The Popularity And History Of Parakeets

For many years, budgerigars, or parakeets, have been a preferred option for avian enthusiasts. These birds are native to Australia, and because of their good climatic and environmental adaptations, they are a flexible choice for farming. They are popular pets all around the globe because of their colorful plumage and capacity to imitate speech and noises.

Parakeets are well-known for being wonderful companions for both novice and experienced bird keepers due to their low maintenance requirements and endearing nature. The increasing demand for parakeets, together with their capacity for reproduction, makes parakeet farming a feasible and lucrative endeavor.

Knowing the Fundamentals of Parakeet Farming

Understanding parakeets' fundamental requirements and behaviors is crucial to raising them properly. These birds need certain circumstances to be healthy, happy, and successful breeders. Everything from their food requirements to their housing needs will be covered in this section.

Environment and housing

Clean, well-ventilated spaces with plenty of natural light are ideal for parakeet growth. Their well-being is greatly impacted by the size of the cage or aviary. Despite their tiny size, parakeets are energetic birds that need room to soar and exercise. Larger cages or aviaries are better for farming since they provide greater space for more birds to dwell in comfort. To provide them with mental and physical stimulation, it is essential to provide them with toys, swings, and perches.

Temperature and Lighting Requirements

Although they can tolerate a lot of temperatures, parakeets prefer those between 65°F and 85°F. Temperature swings may be dangerous, so it's critical to keep things stable. For their well-being, adequate illumination is essential, particularly when it comes to exposure to natural sunshine. If there is a lack of natural light, you may want to use full-spectrum lights to simulate sunlight, which will help them stay healthy overall and manage their circadian cycle.

Nutrition and Feeding

The secret to a healthy parakeet farm is a balanced diet. Although fresh fruits, veggies, and grains make up the majority of a parakeet's diet, a diverse diet will guarantee that they obtain all the nutrients they need. Another great dietary option is parakeet-specific pellets, which provide balanced nutrients in each mouthful. There should always be fresh, clean water accessible.

Providing calcium-rich supplements like cuttlebone aids in the maintenance of robust beaks and bones. To prevent shortages and health problems, it is essential to keep an eye on their diet and make sure they consume a variety of foods.

Advantages Of Keeping Parakeets

Whether you are breeding parakeets for the market, keeping them as pets, or utilizing them for educational reasons,

there are many advantages to raising parakeets. They are a very sought-after bird for a variety of uses because of their amiable disposition, simplicity of maintenance, and ability to procreate.

Cost-effective and Low-maintenance

When compared to other forms of animal husbandry, the little care required for parakeet farming is one of its most alluring features. Large quantities of room or intricate feeding schedules are not necessary for parakeets.

They usually remain healthy and content as long as they have frequent contact, balanced food, and a clean environment

 Because of this, parakeet farming is a great choice for novices or anybody wishing to launch a small-scale bird farming business.

Maintaining a parakeet also comes at a reasonable cost. The primary expenses for your pet, once you have built up their home with the appropriate cages, perches, and feeding supplies, are food, supplements, and infrequent vet visits.

Possibility of Reproduction

Because they reproduce so easily, parakeet farming may be quite lucrative. Parakeets may breed numerous times a year and produce multiple offspring in each clutch under the correct circumstances. This enables farmers to swiftly increase the size of their flock or market young parakeets to pet shops or private buyers.

But breeding has to be done with caution. To prevent problems like inbreeding or passing on genetic abnormalities, it is essential to make sure the birds are in excellent condition and that breeding couples are carefully chosen based on genetics and health.

Demand in the Pet Industry and Companionship

Many people consider parakeets to be among the greatest companion birds for both individuals and families. Their sociable, lively disposition and capacity to establish connections with people make them well-liked companion animals. The profitability of parakeet farming is driven by the increasing demand for parakeets as pets.

Farmers may profit from the pet industry by raising healthy, well-behaved parakeets. When it comes to hand-raised parakeets that are used for human contact, a lot of people are ready to spend more. This creates chances for providing services including training, accessories, and maintenance guidance in addition to selling birds.

Popular Breeds Of Parakeets For Farming

Selecting the appropriate breed is crucial for establishing and succeeding with a parakeet farm. There are several breeds of parakeets to choose from, and each has unique traits, hues, and habits. Some may be perfect for pet owners seeking certain features, while others may be better suited for breeding.

The common parakeet, or budgerigar

Known by most as just "budgie," the budgerigar is the most well-liked and well-known breed of parakeet. Beginner farmers might choose budgerigars because of their lively colors and fun nature. They are popular in both the pet market and among avian hobbyists because of their ease of breeding and upkeep.

Budgies are little birds that average 7 inches in length. They are colored green, blue, yellow, and white, among other colors. Their hardiness and modest size make them a great place to start parakeet farming.

Alexandrine Parakeet

A bigger type of parakeet, the Alexandrine is distinguished by its vivid green plumage and scarlet beak. For individuals looking for bigger, more social parakeet species, these birds are a popular option since they are clever and can be taught to imitate speech.

However, compared to lesser types like budgies, Alexandrine parakeets need more room and care. They are better suitable for seasoned bird farmers or those wishing to specialize in bigger parakeet species due to their greater size and more complicated care requirements.

Ringneck Parakeet of India

Another well-liked breed that is well-known for its lovely coloring and ability to communicate is the Indian Ringneck parakeet. These medium-sized birds have brilliant green, blue, or yellow feathers, and the males notably have a characteristic ring around their necks. They may develop close relationships with their carers and are perceptive and clever.

Raising Indian Ringnecks might be a little more difficult because of their independent and even obstinate attitude. If farmers are looking for a more visually attractive and engaged parakeet species, they are a rewarding breed.

The Quaker Parakeet

Monk parakeets, or Quaker parakeets, are yet another well-liked option for farming. These are medium-sized to tiny birds that are renowned for their playfulness and intelligence. When properly taught, Quaker parakeets may become great mimics and acquire a huge vocabulary.

Unlike many other parakeet varieties that utilize nest boxes, Quakers construct elaborate nests, which sets them apart from other breeds. Their delightful demeanor and simplicity of training make them a valued breed in the parakeet farming industry, but they do need special housing requirements and a more focused approach to breeding.

Farming parakeets is an exciting and fulfilling hobby with many advantages. You may effectively grow healthy and happy parakeets and take advantage of the numerous benefits that come with farming these endearing animals by being aware of the fundamental requirements of these birds and choosing the breed that best suits your objectives.

4o

CHAPTER TWO

Organizing Your Parakeet's Aviary

Although enjoyable, raising parakeets needs careful planning and execution, especially with an aviary setup. The habitat that parakeets reside in has a significant impact on their behavior, health, and ability to reproduce. We'll look at the essential elements of building the ideal aviary for your birds in this chapter. You'll discover all the necessary components to create an environment where your parakeets may flourish, from picking the ideal spot to making sure there is enough ventilation and safety.

Selecting The Ideal Site For Your Aviary

When starting a parakeet farm, choosing a place for your aviary is crucial. Because parakeets are sensitive to their surroundings, choosing the ideal location will have a big influence on both their production and well-being.

Closeness to the House

How near the aviary is to your house should be one of your initial priorities. It is handy to keep it close by for routine maintenance and observation. Keeping your birds nearby also helps shield them from apex predators and inclement weather. But putting it too near to a busy home may expose the birds to too much noise, which would make them anxious.

Shade and Sunlight

For optimal health, parakeets need exposure to natural sunshine, particularly for the creation of vitamin D, which is crucial for healthy bones. Place your aviary so that it receives enough sunshine throughout the day, but also make sure that there is enough shade.

They will be comfortable in milder weather and avoid overheating in the summer with a combination of sun and shade.

Defence Against the Elements

The best place for the aviary is somewhere that protects it from strong winds, torrential rain, and bitter cold. The best location for the aviary might provide some natural protection if it is next to a windbreak,

such as a wall or some trees. Furthermore, stay away from low-lying places that are prone to floods or dampness since moisture might harm your birds' health.

Utility Access

Select a spot with simple access to power if you want to add heating or lights. Similarly, it will be simpler to keep things clean and provide the birds access to clean drinking water if you live close to a water source.

Types of Cages and Aviaries

Selecting the kind of aviary or cage that will work best for your parakeet farm comes next, once you've determined where the greatest place for your aviary is. Depending on your available space, financial constraints, and the number of birds you want to keep, there are a variety of alternatives available, each with unique advantages.

Aviaries: Indoor vs. Outdoor

Your parakeets will have a more enriched habitat in an outside aviary where they may take advantage of the natural light and fresh air. To resist weather and predators, they do, however, need a stronger structure. Conversely, indoor aviaries provide you with more control over the birds' habitat, particularly with regard to humidity and temperature. They need more money spent on artificial lighting and ventilation, but they are less susceptible to outside hazards.

Visit-By Aviaries

If you want to maintain a lot of birds or if you want convenient access for cleaning, feeding, and interacting with the parakeets, a walk-in aviary is a great choice. The birds have more room to soar and play in these aviaries since they are spacious enough for you to walk in and around. If you want to produce parakeets on a big scale, walk-in aviaries are very helpful since they let the birds behave more as they would in the wild.

Aircraft Cages

Flight cages provide a reasonable compromise between space economy and giving birds ample freedom to soar for people with restricted space. Although they are not as spacious as walk-in aviaries, flight cages are nonetheless big enough to accommodate a parakeet's innate need to fly. They are often a more cost-effective choice for inexperienced parakeet growers and may be used both inside and outdoors.

Supplies for Aeries

Take into consideration the materials you choose or utilize to create your aviary. To avoid degradation, the building should be composed of treated wood or metals resistant to rust. There should be tiny enough openings in the mesh or wire to keep rodents and snakes out. Choose stainless steel mesh instead of galvanized metal, since the zinc in it may be hazardous to birds.

Ensuring Safety And Appropriate Ventilation

To protect your parakeets' well-being, it's important to give careful consideration to ventilation and safety measures after deciding on the aviary's location and design. These elements are essential to keeping your birds' habitat healthy and conducive to their growth.

The Significance Of Airflow

For any aviary, enough ventilation is essential. The accumulation of dangerous gases like ammonia, which might result from bird droppings, is prevented by adequate ventilation. Additionally, it aids in temperature regulation, particularly in warm or muggy circumstances. Your parakeets may have respiratory issues in the aviary if there is insufficient airflow, which may cause stuffiness.

Mechanical vs. Natural ventilation

Selecting between mechanical and natural ventilation will depend on whether your aviary is inside or outside. Natural airflow is a common need for outdoor aviaries, and it may be improved by adding vents or mesh walls. If an indoor aviary is located in a humid or poorly ventilated area, mechanical ventilation equipment, like as exhaust fans or air conditioners, may be necessary.

Safety Points to Remember

When creating an aviary, safety should be your first concern. Due to their tiny size and sensitive nature, parakeets are susceptible to threats from the environment and from predators. Make sure the aviary is protected from predators first. This entails having doors that fit securely and making use of sturdy materials that are difficult for critters like raccoons, snakes, or even neighborhood cats to get through.

Stopping Escapes

Due to their agility, parakeets may quickly flee from an aviary if there are any openings or weak points. Make sure that any apertures, such as feeding hatches or doors, are firmly secured and that any wire or mesh is put in the right place. One effective design to stop escapes is a double-door entrance system, where one door opens to a tiny contained space before opening the main aviary door.

Defending Against Insects

Protection against pests like insects and rodents is another factor to take into account. Mice and rats may attempt to get inside the aviary in search of food and may spread illnesses. Make sure food is kept in pest-proof containers and use fine-mesh wire to keep bugs out.

A well-designed aviary, proper ventilation, strategic placement, and safety precautions can all help your parakeet farm flourish. A more prosperous parakeet farming endeavor and healthier, happier birds are the results of careful planning in these areas.

CHAPTER THREE

Choosing Well-Being Parakeets

A crucial first step in launching a parakeet farming operation is choosing healthy birds. Your success will be greatly impacted by the quality and health of the parakeets you pick, whether you're farming for sale, as pets, or for breeding.

To help you make the best selections for your farm, we'll go into detail in this part about how to recognize healthy parakeets, comprehend their behavior and temperament, and take age and gender into account.

Recognising Well-Being Parakeets

Recognizing healthy birds is one of the most crucial abilities to acquire when beginning a parakeet farm. A successful flock of parakeets starts with healthy birds since they live longer, reproduce better, and need less medical attention.

Outward Look

Smooth feathers, clean nostrils, and bright, clear eyes are signs of a healthy parakeet. Their glossy, well-preened feathers show that they take careful care of their feathers. The cleanliness and absence of droppings in the vent, located under the tail, is an indication of a healthy digestive system in birds. Their feet and beaks should also be free of ulcers, swelling, and enlargement. Any swelling, abnormalities, or discoloration might be signs of underlying medical issues.

Examine the parakeets' posture carefully while choosing one. A parakeet in good health perches boldly and stands tall, moving in balanced motions. Birds who breathe heavily, seem languid, or perch for long periods of time with ruffled feathers may be sick.

Voice and Sound

A parakeet's vocalizations might potentially provide information about its health. Active and communicative parakeets are usually in good health. Even if every bird has a different voice, an absolute silence might be unsettling. On the other hand, frequent sneezing, wheezing, or raspy breathing might be signs of respiratory issues, which are prevalent in birds housed in unsuitable conditions.

Habits of Eating and Drinking

A parakeet in good health should be well-fed and consistently consume water. Keep an eye out for birds that stop feeding or suddenly lose weight, since these may be signs of disease. Additionally, their droppings have to have a well-formed appearance, with a white outside and a black core. A poop that is watery, discolored, or smells bad is a symptom of digestive problems and may be an indication of an underlying illness.

Recognizing the Temperament and Behaviour of Parakeets

When choosing birds for farming, it's crucial to consider a parakeet's behavior and temperament in addition to its physical condition. Since each parakeet has a unique personality, you may create a flock of well-adjusted, physically healthy birds by identifying positive behavioral patterns in them.

Social Communication

Being gregarious birds, parakeets' social interactions may reveal a lot about their temperament and general health. Parakeets in good health show curiosity and interest in their surroundings. They should chirp contentedly, investigate their environment, and engage with other birds in the flock. Birds that withdraw from social interactions or behave violently against people might be ill, anxious, or experiencing behavioral problems.

Levels of Activity

Parakeets in good health take pleasure in flying, climbing, and engaging in playtime with toys. They should routinely exercise their legs and wings by moving about the aviary or cage. Birds that exhibit low activity levels or prolonged spells of inactivity may be sick or miserable. It's also important to take into account how they respond to human contact; even if they are not completely domesticated, healthy birds may exhibit interest in people.

Indicators of Stress

Parakeets that exhibit behavioral signs of stress include biting, pacing incessantly, and plucking of feathers. Certain stress-related behaviors may indicate health issues, but they may also be connected to unsatisfactory living circumstances or a lack of stimulation. To avoid stress-related problems in your flock, make sure the environment in which your birds are kept is cozy and stimulating.

Considerations For Age And Gender

Age and gender are crucial aspects to take into account when choosing parakeets for farming. These factors will affect the bird's long-term viability for breeding or selling in addition to its immediate health.

The parakeet's age

For farming, young parakeets are usually the best option, particularly if you want to breed them. Young birds are often more gregarious and more adept at adjusting to unfamiliar surroundings. Six to twelve-month-old birds are thought to be the perfect age for selection since they have outgrown the vulnerable fledgling period but still have many years of potential for reproducing.

If properly cared for, older parakeets may also be excellent candidates, especially for reproducing. However, it's crucial to carefully evaluate an older bird's condition before making a purchase since they could be less able to reproduce and may be more susceptible to health problems.

Selection of Gender

Your agricultural objectives will determine the gender of your parakeets. You'll need a balanced male-to-female ratio if you're breeding. Because parakeets are sexually dimorphic, men and females may be identified by the fleshy region above their beak or cere. Usually, females have a brown or beige cere, whereas males have a blue cere.

While females might be more territorial, males are often more talkative and gregarious, which makes them preferable for farming aimed towards pets. But each bird is different, and some females may be just as gregarious as males. Ensuring the health of both genders is crucial for breeding, as either parent's illness might cause issues with reproduction.

Viability of Reproduction

Take into account the birds' reproductive viability before choosing them for breeding. The ideal breeding ages for parakeets are between one and four years old, while both male and female parakeets achieve sexual maturity at roughly six months. After this age, a bird's fertility may decline and it may produce fewer healthy babies. When choosing mating couples, it is crucial to look for indicators of excellent reproductive health, such as glossy, smooth feathers and energetic behavior.

Choosing healthy parakeets for your agricultural endeavor is a complex procedure that takes into account factors like age and gender in addition to a close examination of behavior, temperament, and physical condition. Selecting birds that are fit, well-adjusted, and appropriate for your farming objectives can provide the groundwork for a prosperous and profitable parakeet farm.

CHAPTER FOUR

Nutrition And Feeding

The Basic Dietary Needs For Parakeets

Knowing the Dietary Requirements for Parakeets

Budgerigars, another name for parakeets, are colorful, energetic birds that need a well-balanced diet to survive. To maintain their lifespan and good health, they have very precise nutritional requirements that must be satisfied. Parakeets eat a variety of foods in the wild, but mostly seeds, fruits, vegetables, and sometimes insects. For best health, pet parakeets, however, often need a more regulated diet.

Vital Components for Parakeets

Essential elements like proteins, carbs, lipids, vitamins, and minerals must be abundant in a parakeet's diet. Proteins are essential for the formation of feathers, growth, and general health. They get the energy they need from carbohydrates to maintain their busy lifestyle. Though in lower quantities, fats are essential for energy and for keeping feathers and skin healthy. Minerals like calcium and vitamins are crucial for maintaining healthy bones and warding off illness.

Meal Timings and Portion Sizes

To match their normal eating habits, parakeets should be given short, regular meals throughout the day. It's crucial to provide a well-balanced mixture of seeds and pellets, with the latter serving as the main food source. Supplements containing seeds are OK, but no more than 20–30% of the diet should consist of them. Regular inclusion of fresh fruits and vegetables is also recommended. Refrain from overfeeding as it might result in obesity and other health problems.

Typical Foods And Supplements
Pellets and Seed Mixes

Although a high-quality seed mix offers vital nutrients, a parakeet's diet shouldn't consist just of it. Choose a blend that contains several types of seeds, such as sunflower, canary, and millet. The main source of nourishment for your parakeet should be pellets as they provide a better balanced diet. They are made to provide every necessary nutrient in the right amounts.

Produce and Fruits

If you want to gain more vitamins and minerals, you need to eat fresh fruits and vegetables. Provide a range of alternatives, such as fruits and vegetables (carrots, apples, berries, and leafy greens like spinach and kale). Wash every vegetable well to get rid of any pollutants or pesticides. Fruit pits and avocados should not be given to them since they are poisonous to birds.

Supplements of vitamins and calcium

For parakeets, calcium is essential, particularly for females to avoid egg-binding. Give out calcium-rich materials like mineral blocks or cuttlebone. Additionally, vitamin supplements could be required, particularly if the food of your bird is monotonous. To ascertain if supplements are required and at what dose, speak with a veterinarian.

Averting Dangerous Foods
Avoid These Toxic Foods

For parakeets, certain meals may be fatal or very toxic. Steer clear of chocolate, coffee, alcohol, and meals high in sugar or salt. Foods that may be poisonous include garlic, onions, and several kinds of nuts. To avoid health problems, make sure your parakeet's food is devoid of these dangerous ingredients.

Safe Food Preparation

Food should always be prepared with caution, and no additions or seasonings that might endanger your bird should be used. Cooking with oils or fats might cause intestinal distress in parakeets. Therefore, avoid using them. To further prevent choking dangers, make sure that any food that is provided is chopped into the proper portions.

Keeping an eye on and modifying diet

Make sure the food is fulfilling your parakeet's requirements by keeping a regular eye on their weight and general health. See a vet if you see any symptoms of disease or behavioral changes in your pet so that you may modify their food. The secret to a healthy and happy parakeet is to provide them with a varied and balanced diet.

CHAPTER FIVE

Raising Parakeets

Expanding your flock and gaining knowledge about the reproductive habits of these vibrant birds might be two benefits of breeding parakeets. Comprehending mating and pairing procedures, erecting suitable nest boxes, and giving eggs and hatchlings the finest care are all necessary for successful reproduction. This comprehensive guide will walk you through every stage of the procedure.

Techniques For Mating And Pairing
Choosing Breeding Pairs

A successful breeding program depends on selecting the appropriate breeding pairings. Choose adult, healthy parakeets first. It is recommended that both genders be at least 6-12 months old. Make sure the birds are clear of parasites and illnesses since these might negatively impact their ability to reproduce. To guarantee the health and vigor of the progeny, seek complementing features when choosing couples, such as vivid plumage and excellent physical condition.

Presenting pairs

Careful preparation is needed when a new pair of parakeets is introduced. Put the birds in an area that is neutral and where none of them has claimed territory. This lessens the likelihood of hostilities and territorial conflicts. Keep a careful eye on how they interact. Keep an eye out for behaviors that indicate a relationship is developing, including preening, feeding, and snuggling close. If the birds aren't getting along, think about trying alternative pairings or returning them after a little break.

Promoting the Mating Behaviour

Establish a setting that resembles the parakeets' breeding season in order to promote mating. This entails offering healthy food, plenty of light, and a cozy, stress-free atmosphere. If a parakeet feels safe and fed, they are more inclined to mate. Provide a diverse, nutrient-dense diet to maintain the health of the reproductive system.

A range of perches and toys may also aid in encouraging bonding and enhancing natural behaviors.

Comprehending Mating Customs

During courting, one may witness the particular mating rituals that parakeets follow. To entice the female, the male would often put on a show by bobbing his head, singing, and puffing out his feathers.

In response, the female could exhibit her own curiosity by bending in the direction of the male and fluttering her wings. When the birds are ready to mate, you may tell by watching these behaviors.

Care And Setup For Nesting Boxes
Selecting an Appropriate Nesting Box

Since it gives the female a secure place to deposit her eggs and rear her young, the nesting box is crucial to a successful breeding operation. Choose a box that is the right size for parakeets, which is typically 6 by 6 by 9 inches. A detachable side panel or lid would make cleaning and observation much easier. To avoid overheating, make sure it is constructed of sturdy, non-toxic materials and has enough ventilation.

Nesting Box Positioning Correctly

In an area of the aviary or cage where the birds feel comfortable and peaceful, place the nesting box. Do not put it in a busy place where there will be a lot of noise or bustle since this can stress the birds. The location of the box should be such that it is conveniently accessible, while still shielded from breezes and direct sunlight.

While laying and incubating her eggs, the female will feel more at ease and secure if her location is steady and secure.

Keeping Things Tidy

For the sake of the health of the breeding couple and their offspring, the nesting box must be kept clean. Check the box often for evidence of food remnants or droppings, and wipe it with a light disinfectant if necessary. To keep the surroundings sanitary, replace any dirty nesting material, such as wood shavings or shredded paper. Maintaining a clean nesting box keeps the birds healthy and helps stop the spread of sickness.

Keeping an eye on nesting activity

Once the female parakeet begins to use the nesting box, pay careful attention to her behavior. Keep an eye out for indications of egg laying, such as longer time spent in the box and activity related to nesting. During this period, try not to upset the birds too much since touching them often might stress them out. To make sure the eggs are being properly cared for and that nothing is wrong, check the box once in a while.

Taking Care Of Hatchlings And Eggs
Time of Incubation

Usually, parakeet eggs take 18 to 21 days to incubate. The female will spend most of this time in the nesting box, periodically flipping and warming the eggs. Make sure the environment is steady and unaltered since changes in humidity or temperature might have an impact on how the embryos grow. A steady diet high in protein and calcium will help the female mature her eggs and maintain her overall health.

Taking Care of Eggs and Hatchlings

To lessen anxiety and avoid mishaps, handle the eggs and hatchlings as little as possible. Gently and rapidly inspect the eggs if necessary. If you want to keep an eye on how the eggs are developing, candle them with a torch. Upon hatching, the chicks need continual warmth and attention since they are so delicate at first. To ensure the chicks stay warm, make sure the nesting box is well insulated.

Growth and feeding

The chicks' dietary requirements will rise as they become bigger. For a while, the parents would only give them food that they had regurgitated. As they become older, you may add soft, nutrient-dense meals to their diet, including finely chopped fruits and vegetables. Keep a careful eye on the chicks' development to make sure they are growing and gaining weight as intended. Increasing their protein and calcium intake will benefit their general health and bone growth.

Getting Ready for Weaning

The last phase of a chick's growth before they become autonomous is weaning. Gradually introduce solid meals, presenting a range of fruits, grains, and seeds. Make sure the chicks are making a seamless transition from their parents' care to self-feeding by keeping an eye on how they adjust to these new meals. When they are eating on their own and completely weaned, you may begin getting them ready for adoption or blending them into the main flock.

CHAPTER SIX

Parakeet Medical Services

There is more to caring for parakeets than simply giving them food and a cage. Their lifespan and happiness depend on maintaining their health and well-being. Understanding prevalent ailments, identifying symptoms of sickness, and maintaining proper cleanliness and grooming habits are all part of proper health care. This section explores each of these facets in detail, offering a thorough how-to manual for those new to parakeet farming.

Common Parakeet Illnesses And How To Avoid Them

1. Summary of Typical Parakeet Illnesses

Like any pets, parakeets may have a variety of illnesses. Understanding these prevalent illnesses facilitates early diagnosis and treatment. Typical ailments in parakeets consist of:

• Psittacosis: A bacterial ailment that may afflict both people and birds, it is sometimes referred to as parrot fever. Parakeet symptoms include changes in droppings, tiredness, and respiratory problems. It's critical to maintain a clean environment and keep sick birds at bay.

• Avian polyomavirus: This virus, especially in young parakeets, may be lethal. Feather loss, low-quality feathers, and puffiness are among the symptoms. Vaccinations and routine veterinary examinations may help avoid this illness.

• Chlamydiosis: This bacterium-caused illness causes eye infections and respiratory problems. To stop the spread, sick birds must be kept apart and good cleanliness must be maintained.

2. Preventive Actions

Disease prevention comprises a number of crucial actions:

• Routine Veterinary Check-ups: Early illness identification and prevention are facilitated by routine veterinary checkups. Health tests and vaccines may be administered by your veterinarian.

• Clean Environment: Make sure your parakeets' living area is kept tidy. Keep the toys, perches, and cage clean on a regular basis to avoid the growth of parasites and dangerous pathogens.

• Proper Nutrition: Your parakeet's immune system is strengthened with a well-balanced diet. Give them a diverse diet consisting of fruits, veggies, seeds, and pellets.

• Isolation of New Birds: To stop the spread of illness, quarantine new birds before integrating them into your current flock.

Symptoms Of Disease And When To Contact A Vet

1. Identifying Symptoms of Illness

The likelihood of recovery may be greatly increased by early sickness identification. Typical indicators that your parrot could be ill are as follows:

• Change in Droppings: Unusual droppings may be a sign of an infection or gastrointestinal problems. Keep an eye out for variations in hue, texture, or regularity.

• Lethargy: If a parakeet seems abnormally quiet or uninterested, it can be unwell. Parakeets in good health tend to be lively and inquisitive.

• Feather Problems: Unusual feather development, ruffled feathers, or excessive feather loss may all be indicators of health problems.

• Respiratory Issues: Difficulty breathing, wheezing, or nasal discharge are signs of respiratory problems that require immediate attention.

2. When to Seek Veterinary Care

Certain symptoms necessitate a vet visit:

• Persistent Symptoms: If symptoms persist for more than a day or worsen, consult a vet. Delayed treatment can lead to more severe health issues.

• Severe Behavioral Changes: Sudden changes in behavior, such as aggression or excessive hiding, may indicate underlying health problems.

• Injuries: Any signs of injury, such as bleeding or difficulty moving, should be evaluated by a vet immediately.

3. Preparing for the Vet Visit

• Record Symptoms: Documenting symptoms and any changes in behavior helps the vet make an accurate diagnosis.

• • Bring a Sample: For analysis if at all feasible, bring a sample of feathers or droppings.

Basic Personal Care And Hygiene
1. The Value of Personal Care

Your parakeet's general health and well-being depend on regular grooming. Grooming them on a regular basis improves your relationship with them and helps preserve their physical health.

2. Taking Care of Feathers

• Bathing: To maintain clean and healthy feathers, parakeets need frequent showers. Offer a misting bottle or a little bowl of water. Make sure the water is chemical-free and at room temperature.

• Feather Trimming: Examine feathers often and cut them as needed. Overgrown feathers may make it difficult to move and fly. Trimming should be done carefully; if in doubt, see a veterinarian.

3. Take Care of Your Nails and Beak

• Nail trimming: The long, sharp nails of parakeets may develop and cause pain or damage. Regular nail trimming will keep your nails from growing too long. To cut nails on birds, use specialized tools and take care not to cut too near too the quick.

• Maintenance of the Beak: Over time, parakeets' beaks naturally deteriorate, but sometimes they may grow abnormally or overgrow. Give them natural perches and chew toys to aid with beak maintenance. See a vet if you see any anomalies in the beak.

4. Practices of Hygiene

• Cage Cleaning: Keep the cage, together with its perches, toys, and food bowls, clean on a regular basis. To stop germs from growing, replace dirty bedding with new material.

• Health Checks: Perform routine health examinations to keep an eye out for any changes or problems. Take quick action if you see any indications of mites, lice, or other parasites.

5. Mental Health and Enrichment

• Enrichment of the Environment: Create an engaging space with toys, perches, and chances for socializing. Boredom and associated health problems may be avoided with enrichment.

• Social Interaction: To promote mental health and social ties, spend time each day with your parakeet. You may maintain cerebral stimulation in your parakeet via interactive play and instruction.

Understanding common ailments, seeing symptoms of sickness, and keeping appropriate grooming habits are all important components of proper parakeet health care. By being knowledgeable and proactive, you can guarantee the health and happiness of your parakeets.

CHAPTER SEVEN

Teaching And Taking Care Of Parakeets

Teaching Simple Commands And Tricks

Not only can teaching your parakeet simple tricks and orders prolong its life, but it also fortifies the relationship between you and your feathery companion. This section will walk you through the best ways to teach your parakeet basic skills so that you and your bird have a happy and fulfilling time together.

1. Initially, using positive reinforcement

Effective training is built on the foundation of positive reinforcement. This entails giving your parakeet attention, praise, or food whenever it demonstrates a desirable behavior. Start by choosing a little, healthful treat that your parakeet enjoys, such as a tiny seed or a piece of fruit. Small enough to be rapidly digested, the goodie should provide numerous incentives throughout training sessions.

2. Teaching Commands to Step Up and Step Down

An essential skill for managing and teaching your parakeet is the step-up **command**. Say "step up" to your parakeet as you urge it to step onto your finger by carefully placing your finger or a perch under its foot to teach it this order. Give the bird a treat and some praise right away. Similar instructions apply to the step-down command, which is to encourage the bird to move off your finger or the perch. Since it could take many sessions for your parakeet to learn these instructions, consistency, and patience are essential.

3. Presenting Fundamental Techniques

You may add more advanced tricks like "wave" or "spin" if your parakeet is used to the step-up and step-down orders. To teach your parakeet the wave trick, hold a treat over its head and softly tap its foot. Give it the treat and some vocal praise as soon as it lifts a foot to reach for it. Hold a reward close to your parakeet's head and use the spin trick to train it to follow the treat by spinning in a circle. Your parakeet will eventually come to identify these actions with the rewards.

4. Patience and consistency

A key component of training is consistency. To keep your parakeet interested and prevent weariness, conduct brief, frequent training sessions, preferably lasting between five and ten minutes. Even if there isn't much development, wrap off each session with a cheerful attitude. Remember that every bird learns differently, therefore patience is key. If difficulties arise, stand back and review the fundamental instructions or consult with knowledgeable parakeet trainers.

5. Preventing Typical Errors

Steer clear of frequent training errors like punishing or becoming frustrated. Because they are sensitive birds, parakeets react best to praise. Take a pause and give it another go later if your bird seems anxious or uninterested. Make sure your parakeet can concentrate on learning by holding training sessions in a calm, distraction-free setting.

Building Relationships And Trust With Your Parakeet

Fundamental elements of effective parakeet farming include developing a relationship of trust and bonding with your bird. In addition to improving your parakeet's health, a trustworthy connection makes training and managing them more pleasurable. This section looks at how to build a close relationship with your parakeet.

1. Establishing a Secure and Cosy Environment

A connection built on trust is based on a safe and secure environment. Make sure the cage housing your parakeet is roomy, tidy, and furnished with toys, perches, and dishes for food and water. The cage should be placed in a peaceful environment where your parakeet may see everyday events without being overstimulated. Introduce new things or modifications to the surroundings gradually to prevent creating tension.

2. Having a Good Time Together

Having regular interactions is crucial to developing trust. Every day, spend time conversing and playing with your parakeet. When conversing with your bird, talk in a soothing, quiet tone and refrain from making abrupt motions that might frighten it. To help your parakeet get comfortable and used to being around you, gently extend your finger or provide a perch for it to land on.

3. Providing Sweets and Incentives

Treats are important for fostering bonds. Give your parakeet little treats throughout interactions and as a reward for good behavior. By providing positive reinforcement, you may encourage your parakeet to link you with happy memories. To maintain a balanced diet and avoid overfeeding, be cautious of the amount and type of goodies you consume.

4. Recognising Body Language

Understanding the body language used by parakeets to communicate helps strengthen relationships. Keep an eye out for indicators of calm, such as lightly vocalized, relaxed posture, and fluffed feathers. On the other hand, fast flapping of the wings, grinding of the beak, or defensive actions are indicators of stress or discomfort. In order to provide a comforting and encouraging atmosphere, pay attention to your parakeet's body language.

5. Respect and Patience

Trust must be earned gradually and patiently. Recognize your parakeet's limits and refrain from pressuring them to engage. Be prepared for obstacles and let your bird come to you at its own speed. Honor little victories and keep creating a caring and supportive atmosphere.

Managing And Conversing Advice

A well-mannered and amiable parakeet requires careful handling and socialization. This section offers helpful advice on how to care for your parakeet and encourage socialization.

1. Modest Handling Methods

Use calm, soft motions while handling your parakeet. Steer clear of abrupt or jerky movements and approach the bird cautiously. Relax and put your hand or finger in the cage;

your parakeet will come to you. When raising your parakeet, make sure its body is supported evenly and it feels comfortable and safe.

2. Progressive Socialisation

In order to increase your parakeet's comfort and confidence, socialization entails introducing it to a variety of stimuli and situations. Gradually expand your exposure to novel environments by starting with brief, supervised encounters. In order to avoid overstimulating your parakeet, gradually introduce it to new people, places, and items.

3. Promoting Harmonious Interactions

Use rewards and praise to promote good relationships while handling and socializing. Give your parakeet a treat or vocal encouragement for its peaceful and contented behavior. Reward or punishment should be avoided since they may undermine the trust you've worked so hard to establish.

4. Identifying Stress Signs

When touching and socializing, keep an eye out for any indications of stress, such as flailing wings, puffed feathers, or vocalizations. Take a pause and give your parakeet some time to settle down if it seems uncomfortable before interacting with it again. A happy, stress-free atmosphere is essential for effective socialization.

5. Playing Interactive Games

Engaging in interactive play with your parakeet is a great way to improve your relationship and provide cerebral stimulation. Make use of games and activities that promote discovery and communication, such as swings, mirrors, and foraging toys. Playfully and gently engage with your parakeet to keep them interested and active.

CHAPTER EIGHT

Parakeet Communication And Behaviour

Recognising Body Language And Vocalisations

Being very talkative birds, parakeets need a novice in parakeet farming to interpret their vocalizations and body language. Parakeets primarily communicate by vocalizations, which range from chirps and whistles to squawks and screams. Depending on the circumstances in which they are produced, each sound might have a distinct meaning.

Voices

1. Whistling and chirping are often indications of a contented parakeet. A parakeet will often chirp while it is engaging with its surroundings or its owner. Whistling may also be a sign of happiness and playfulness for the parakeet. A

parakeet may be imitating noises it hears around it if it begins to whistle melodies.

2. Screaming and squawking are examples of loud, sudden sounds that indicate irritation or discomfort. Overwhelming squawking or shrieking in a parakeet may indicate a problem, such as discomfort in the surroundings, inattention, or health problems. It's critical to assess the environment and ascertain if these noises are sporadic or persistent since loud vocalizations that continue over time may point to a more serious issue.

3. Speech Mimicking: Parakeets are well-known for their capacity to imitate many sounds, including human speech. This kind of behavior often suggests that they feel at ease and acclimated in their surroundings. Both the bird and its owner may benefit from the enjoyable and rewarding experience of teaching them to talk or imitate sounds.

Body Language

1. Feather Fluffing: A parakeet's feather fluffing may indicate contentment or calm. When a bird feels safe and at ease, or to control their body temperature, they often fluff their feathers.

2. Tail Wagging: Waving the tail may convey agitation or excitement. Your parakeet may be indicating that it is thrilled about something, such as seeing a favorite toy or reward if it is waving its tail quickly.

3. Head bobbing: When the parakeet is pleased or attempting to socialize with others, it may exhibit this indication of pleasure. But if it starts to get out of hand, it can be a sign of something more that needs to be looked at.

4. Preening and Bowing: To convey confidence and love, parakeets preen their feathers and bend their heads. This behavior is indicative of a good connection between the bird and its

carer and may be a means for the birds to bond with their owners.

Dealing With Behavioural Issues

Vigilant monitoring and proactive behavior modification are necessary to identify and resolve behavioral issues in parakeets. Like other pets, parakeets sometimes display behaviors that could appear troublesome, but these problems are often manageable with the appropriate techniques.

Typical Behavioural Problems

1. Aggression: Parakeets that are aggressive may bite, lunge, or vocalize loudly. Fear, territorial tendencies, or frustration may all cause this behavior. It's critical to identify the underlying causes of aggressiveness and treat them with positive reinforcement and progressive desensitization.

2. Feather Plucking: Plucking feathers may indicate medical problems, boredom, or stress.

Make sure the parakeet has plenty of toys and socializing chances in a setting that is exciting. See an avian veterinarian to rule out any underlying health issues if feather plucking continues.

3. Loud Vocalisations: While occasional vocalization is acceptable, loud noises might be upsetting. Evaluating the causes of loud vocalizations is essential. Make sure the parakeet isn't lonely or bored, and look for any environmental changes that could be stressing it out.

4. Insufficient Socialisation: Insufficiently socialized parakeets may display timid or reclusive tendencies. Spending quality time with your parakeet, playing interactively, and giving positive reinforcement to boost confidence and social engagement are all effective ways to increase social interaction.

Methods and Approaches

1. Behavioural Training: Unwanted behaviors may be changed with the use of positive reinforcement approaches. When your parakeet behaves well, give it food or praise to encourage it to keep up the good work.

2. Environmental Enrichment: Keeping your parakeet occupied and lowering the risk of behavioral issues is possible by providing a stimulating environment with toys, perches, and social contact. To keep kids interested, rotate toys often.

3. Structure and Routine: Creating a regular schedule can reassure your parakeet and lessen behaviors linked to worry. Establishing consistent feeding, play, and sleep patterns helps create a stable atmosphere.

4. Veterinary Consultation: Seek advice from an avian veterinarian if behavioral problems continue despite your best efforts. A specialist may assist in determining if there are any

underlying medical disorders influencing the behavior and provide focused therapy.

Improving Communication With Others

Improving social contact with your parakeet promotes a deep link between you and your pet and is vital to its overall health. As gregarious birds, parakeets enjoy the company and stimulation of their human partners.

Creating a Connection

1. Regular Engagement: Make time each day to engage with your parakeet. Play with it gently sing to it, or engage in other activities. Regular communication improves trust and fortifies your relationship.

2. Training and Tricks: Introducing your parakeet to basic instructions or tricks will greatly improve communication. Start with simple instructions like "step up" and work your

way up to more intricate ones. Use constructive criticism to promote learning.

3. Social Playtime: If at all feasible, give your parakeet the opportunity to interact with other parakeets. Playing socially with other birds may help meet their social demands and keep them from being lonely.

4. Use interactive toys: Foraging or puzzle toys are examples of toys that promote interaction. With the mental stimulation and engagement provided by these toys, your parakeet will exhibit less negative behavior and less boredom.

Establishing an Exciting Ambience

1. Cage Setup: Make sure the cage has enough toys, perches, and climbing frames for your parakeet. Your parakeet will remain active and interested in its surroundings if it is diverse and exciting.

2. Outside of the Cage opportunity: Give your parakeet some opportunity to explore and engage with its environment outside of the cage. Time spent outside the cage under supervision encourages socialization and exercise.

3. Training Sessions: Make time each day for quick training sessions. Target training, recall training, and teaching new behaviors are some examples of these sessions. Training sessions strengthen the link between you and your parakeet and stimulate the mind.

4. Positive Reinforcement: To reward good behavior, provide goodies and praise. Giving your parakeet a treat when it interacts with you or performs well encourages it to carry out these actions again.

84

CHAPTER NINE

Handling The Farm Enterprise

Cost Control And Budgeting

Overview of Budgeting

An efficient budget is essential to a profitable parakeet farming enterprise. Maintaining the profitability of your farm requires careful planning and management of your finances. To start creating a thorough financial plan, include all possible costs and income.

Determining Initial Expenses

Setting up your farm, buying supplies, and getting your first batch of parakeets all count towards your first investment in parakeet farming. Construction or acquisition of an aviary, feeding, and watering systems, cages, and early veterinarian care are among the major costs. Also take into account the expenses of purchasing breeding pairs, which might be greater if you choose uncommon or superior parakeets.

Continuous Operating Expenses

Continual expenses are essential to keeping a business running smoothly. These include food, bedding supplies, utilities (such as power for air conditioning or heating), and routine veterinarian treatment.

 If you want to recruit employees, don't forget to account for labor expenditures in addition to marketing and distribution charges.

Establishing a System for Tracking Finances

Organize your finances by putting in place a financial monitoring system. A basic spreadsheet or accounting program may be used for this. To keep an eye on your cash flow and see any places where you may save money, keep a close eye on all of your receipts and outlays.

Financial Planning And Forecasting

Make financial projections to estimate your future earnings and outlays. This entails projecting future expenses and forecasting revenues using market research and previous data.

To keep on track, occasionally adjust your budget depending on actual performance and market circumstances.

Money-Saving Techniques

Seek ways to save expenses without sacrificing the quality of care for your parakeet. Lowering total expenses may be achieved by buying feed and supplies in bulk, investing in energy-efficient machinery, and haggling with suppliers to get better deals. Saving money may also be achieved by putting effective farm management strategies into practice

Legal and License Requirements

Comprehending the Need for Licensing

You must be aware of local licensing regulations before launching a parakeet farming operation. This might include applying for a business license, a license to breed pets, and perhaps even specialized licenses for keeping and taking care of birds. Verify that you abide by all laws by consulting with the relevant national and local authorities.

Regulations for Health and Safety

For the sake of your parakeets' welfare and legal compliance, your farm has to abide by health and safety requirements.

This entails preserving hygienic conditions, providing sufficient ventilation, and making sure that trash is managed appropriately. Periodic evaluations could be necessary to guarantee adherence.

Legal Aspects of Animal Welfare

According to animal welfare standards, you must provide your parakeets with the right care, which includes enough shelter, food, and medical attention. Learn about the local regulations pertaining to animal welfare in order to stay out of trouble with the law and to make sure your parakeets are happy and well-cared after.

Liability and Insurance

If you want to safeguard your farm from possible threats, think about getting insurance. This may include property insurance to cover damage to your farm or equipment, as well as liability insurance in the event of accidents or injuries. To find out which insurance policies are best for your company, speak with an insurance expert.

Maintaining Documents and Adhering to Regulations

Keep thorough records of every action taken to comply with laws and regulations.

This contains any communication with regulatory organizations as well as records of licenses and inspections. Maintaining organized records is beneficial, and they may come in handy during audits or legal questions.

Selling And Promoting Parakeets
Formulating a Marketing Plan

To sell your parakeets and draw in clients, you need a well-planned marketing approach. Decide who your target customer is. They can be bird lovers, pet retailers, or individual pet owners. Make your marketing strategies appealing to this target market.

Establishing Your Online Identity

It is essential to have an online presence in the modern digital world. Make a polished website that highlights your parakeets' breeding facts, maintenance guidelines, and details. Make use of social media channels to interact with prospective clients, communicate updates, and reach a larger audience.

Partnerships and Networking

Establish connections with nearby veterinarian offices, bird groups, and pet shops. Through networking, you may locate potential customers and get recommendations. Think about cooperating on events or providing these organizations a percentage on sales as a way to work with them for mutual gain.

Distribution and Sales Channels

Choose which sales methods will work best for your parakeets. This might include working with pet retailers, selling directly from your farm, or doing business online. Take into account the distribution procedures, such as packing and shipping, to guarantee that your parakeets arrive undamaged.

Customer Support and Input

Building a devoted clientele requires providing exceptional customer service. Give them concise information on your parakeets, give advice on how to take care of them, and respond to their questions right away. Get client feedback so you can make improvements to your offerings and deal with any problems that may occur.

CHAPTER TEN

Growing Your Farm Of Parakeets

Overview Of Farm Expansion

Investing and strategic planning are necessary for growing your parakeet farm. Not only is it important to increase the number of birds, but it's also important to improve the infrastructure as a whole, guarantee sustainability, and maximize production. Understanding the benefits and difficulties that come with growing your business is essential for successful development.

Evaluating Your Present-Day Functions

Take a close look at your present activities before growing. Examine your current breeding programs, aviary setups, and general farm management. Determine which areas need improvement and what infrastructure or extra resources will be needed. This study can assist you in establishing reasonable objectives and guaranteeing that the foundations of your development strategy are strong.

Creating New Aviaries

When designing additional aviaries, it's important to keep your growing flock's needs in mind and make sure the new areas are suitable for them. The design should prioritize having enough room, good ventilation, and natural light. Think about modular architectures that provide scalability and flexibility. Make sure pests and predators cannot access the aviaries.

Purchasing Devices and Technology

Investing in contemporary machinery and technology may greatly increase your parakeet farm's productivity. In addition to streamlining operations, automated feeding systems, temperature control systems, and monitoring technologies may enhance the health and well-being of your birds. Look into and choose equipment based on your budget and individual requirements.

Planning Your Finances for Growth

Your parakeet farm expansion needs a well-thought-out finance strategy. Determine how much it will cost to construct more aviaries, buy equipment, and hire more workers. Examine your possibilities for finance, including grants, loans, and investors. Make sure that predictions for rising income and spending are part of your financial strategy.

Aspects of Regulation and Compliance to Take into Account

Make sure you abide by local laws and guidelines for farm operations and animal care as you grow. Obtain the licenses and permissions that are required. To prevent any compliance difficulties, study industry best practices and regulatory requirements on a regular basis and follow them.

Expanding Your Aviary
Comprehending the Process of Scaling

There's more to scaling up your aviary than merely adding extra cages. It necessitates a thorough strategy that takes care of your farm's administrative, operational, and physical elements. By scaling up or down appropriately, your farm may accommodate a bigger flock without sacrificing the standard of care.

Making the Most of Space and Arrangement

To scale up, a layout must be optimized. Arrange the new aviary area to optimize productivity and provide convenient access for routine administrative duties.

Take into account adding elements like moveable walls or movable perches to suit various flock sizes and requirements. More space efficiency will make upkeep simpler and improve bird health.

Improving Facilities for Breeding

Improving your breeding facilities is another aspect of scaling up your aviary. To guarantee effective breeding, spend money on top-notch nesting boxes, breeding cages, and monitoring devices. Review and adjust your breeding procedures on a regular basis to preserve genetic variety and increase yield.

Putting Advanced Management Techniques into Practice

When you grow, advanced management strategies may help to optimize processes. Establish mechanisms to monitor the health, egg production, and feed intake of birds.

Analyse data to spot patterns and come to wise judgments. Sustaining high standards also requires staff training on new methods and technology.

Sustaining Quality Assurance

Maintaining quality control becomes more crucial as your aviary expands. Keep a regular eye on the health and welfare of your birds. Put into practice procedures for managing and preventing illness.

 To avoid any possible problems, make sure that every employee complies with hygiene and safety requirements.

Organizing for Potential Growth

By establishing long-term objectives and regularly assessing your scaling plan, you can prepare for future development.

Think about the market's possible prospects and obstacles. Keep up with developments and trends in the industry that may affect your goals for growth.

Diversifying Breeds Of Parakeets

Overview of Breed Diversification

Increasing the variety of breeds of parakeets you raise may improve your farm's appeal and financial success. Providing a range of breeds may accommodate varying consumer inclinations and provide new business prospects. To protect all breeds, diversity has to be carefully planned for and managed.

Investigating Breed Varieties

To start, learn about the unique requirements and traits of various parakeet breeds by doing research on them.

Certain breeds could need particular attention or surroundings. Learn about their food needs, breeding patterns, and any health concerns. With this information, you will be able to provide each breed with the finest care possible.

Changing the aviary conditions

The needs of different breeds may vary with regard to humidity, temperature, and space. Adapt the conditions in your aviary to meet their demands.

For example, some breeds may need bigger cages or certain kinds of materials to build nests. Make sure the layout of your aviary can be easily adjusted to meet the needs of various breeds.

Controlling Genetic Diversities

Maintaining genetic variety is essential to your parakeet breed's health and longevity. Put in place a breeding strategy that discourages inbreeding and encourages genetic variety.

To maintain healthy, vigorous bird populations, regularly assess your breeding methods and make appropriate modifications.

Selling a Variety of Breeds

Promoting a variety of parakeet breeds might draw in a larger clientele. In your marketing brochures, emphasize each breed's unique qualities and advantages.

Provide educational information that informs prospective customers about the traits and maintenance needs of various breeds.

Assessing Demand in the Market

Analyze the market demand for various parakeet breeds on a regular basis. Track consumer preferences and sales patterns to make well-informed choices about which breeds to concentrate on.

Be ready to modify your breeding and marketing plans in response to input from the market and new trends.

Getting Assistance And Assigning Work
Determine Staffing Requirements

Hiring assistance and assigning responsibilities to others become crucial for effective management as your parakeet farm grows. Determine the precise positions and duties that need filling. Think of jobs like breeders, aviary managers, and maintenance personnel. Give each role's criteria and job description a clear definition.

Hiring Talented Personnel

Post job vacancies on several platforms, including industry networks, online job boards, and neighborhood community centers, to attract eligible candidates. Make sure that applicants have the requisite training and experience by conducting in-depth interviews and background investigations. To ensure that new personnel adhere to the norms and procedures of your farm, provide them with training.

Successful Techniques for Delegation

Delegation done well is essential to running an expanding farm. Assign work in accordance with employees' abilities and competencies. Establish a transparent framework for communicating and allocating tasks. To make sure that every project is finished quickly and to a high quality, examine it often and make any necessary adjustments.

Education and Training

To improve the skills and knowledge of your employees, make training and development investments. To keep them informed about industry innovations and best practices, provide resources and continual education. Promoting professional development may enhance output and work happiness.

Keeping an eye on and assessing performance.

Make sure that staff members are doing their jobs well by routinely observing and assessing their performance.

Give constructive criticism and take quick action to resolve any problems. Conduct performance evaluations to evaluate employee contributions and pinpoint areas in need of development.

Creating a Happy Workplace

Maintaining a happy workplace is critical to employee satisfaction and output.

Promote open communication, respect for one another, and collaboration among employees. **To** create an environment that is encouraging and supportive, acknowledge and thank them for their efforts.

CHAPTER ELEVEN

Ethical And Sustainable Farming Methods

Taking Care Of Animal Welfare

In every agricultural business, including parakeet farming, the well-being of the animals comes first. Adopting methods that meet your parakeets' physical and psychological demands is crucial to ensuring their well-being.

1. Giving Enough Room

For parakeets to fly and roam freely, there must be enough room. Enough rooms should be provided in cages for people to walk around and exercise comfortably. Generally speaking, the cage should be at least twice as long and high as the bird's wingspan. Furthermore, think of building aviaries that will allow parakeets to fly in a more organic setting, which will enhance their general well-being.

2. Making Sure You're Eating Right

For parakeets to be healthy, they need a balanced diet. A range of seeds, fruits, vegetables, and specially prepared parakeet pellets should be part of their diet. Food should not include any pollutants, and fresh water should always be accessible. See a veterinarian on a regular basis to make sure your bird food program is meeting their nutritional requirements.

3. Keeping an eye on behavior and health

Behavioral observations and routine health examinations are crucial. Keep an eye out for symptoms of disease or discomfort, like as activity levels, droppings, or changes in plumage. Consult a veterinary specialist for birds right away if there are any health concerns. To further avoid boredom and behavioral issues, provide cerebral stimulation via toys and social engagement.

4. Creating Enriched and Safe Environments

Make sure the habitats you provide for your parakeets are secure and engaging. To keep them occupied, offer them a variety of perches and toys and refrain from putting pesticides or other harmful items in their cages. Foraging and puzzle toys are two examples of enrichment activities that mimic natural behaviors and improve the well-being of the animals.

5. Ethical Guidelines for Breeding

It's important to breed parakeets carefully. Prevent overbreeding, since it may cause health problems and stress in the birds. Make sure that breeding partners are in good condition and that the environments in which their kids are nurtured are supportive. Respect morality and refrain from adding to the issue of pet overpopulation.

Sustainable Farming Methods

By using environmentally friendly techniques, you may lessen your impact on the environment and support sustainable agriculture while raising parakeets. The following are some essential methods:

1. Management of Wastes

An environmentally friendly farm must be maintained with effective waste management. Clean up and compost bird droppings on a regular basis to use as plant fertilizer. Make sure that all garbage is appropriately handled to avoid pollution and harm to the environment.

2. Energy-saving Techniques

To reduce the amount of energy used on your farm, use energy-efficient methods. Make your bird cages' lighting and heating systems more energy-efficient. Think about powering your buildings with alternative energy sources, like solar panels.

3. Sustainable Materials Sourcing

Use resources that come from sustainable sources while establishing and maintaining your parakeet farm. Choose eco-friendly items; for example, use non-toxic cleaning agents and recyclable materials when building cages. Steer clear of goods that worsen the environment or cause deforestation.

4. Conserving Water

Reduce water use by putting conservation measures into practice. Water-efficient methods should be used for cleaning and bird watering. In order to reduce waste and reuse water wherever feasible, think about installing water recycling devices.

5. Encouraging Biodiversity

Incorporate native trees and plants into the landscape of your farm to promote biodiversity. These plants may help local animals and provide your parakeets with natural foraging possibilities. Steer clear of herbicides and chemicals that might damage the ecosystem.

Developing A Credibility For Moral Conduct

Developing a reputation for moral behavior in parakeet farming is advantageous to your company as well as the larger avian community. Here's how you build and preserve a reputation for ethics:

1. Open and Accountable Operations

Be open and honest about your standards and agricultural methods. Inform clients and the

general public about your breeding procedures, environmental initiatives, and policies regarding animal care. Being transparent shows that you value moral behavior and fosters trust.

2. Taking Part in Community Activities

Encourage ethical agricultural methods by interacting with nearby communities and avian lovers. Take part in neighborhood gatherings, provide informative seminars, and cooperate with nearby groups that promote environmental preservation and animal welfare.

3. Acquiring Certifications

Think about earning certifications from reputable groups that emphasize sustainable agricultural methods and animal welfare. Credibility-boosting certifications from organizations that promote ethical farming, like the Humane Society, may attest to your dedication to upholding high standards.

4. Constant Enhancement

Make it a goal to keep improving your agricultural methods. Review and update your rules often to ensure they comply with the most recent environmental and ethical guidelines. To find areas that need improvement, get input from clients, staff members, and industry professionals.

5. Increasing Conscience

Make use of your influence to raise awareness of moral parakeet farming methods. Through blogs, industry magazines, and social media, share your triumphs and experiences. Promote excellent practices and persuade other farmers to use moral and environmentally friendly methods.

Conclusion

Taking Stock of the Parakeet Farming Experience

As we get to the end of this beginner's guide to parakeet farming, it's important to take stock of your experience. Breeding and rearing these colorful and perceptive birds is just one aspect of parakeet farming; other aspects include a dedication to their welfare, a love of avian care, and an investment in providing a healthy habitat for them.

We've covered a wide variety of issues in this book, from controlling the nutrition and health of parakeets to comprehending their behavior and creating an appropriate environment. Every chapter is intended to provide you with the fundamental understanding and useful advice needed to launch your parakeet farming business with success.

Important lessons learned

Let's review some of the important lessons learned from this book:

1. Comprehending Parakeet Behaviour: Establishing a peaceful atmosphere requires an understanding of parakeet behavior. A cozy and engaging environment may be created by taking note of their social demands, communication styles, and innate behaviors.

2. Creating the Perfect Environment: Your parakeets' health and happiness are directly related to their environment. This includes providing stimulating toys and perches, making sure the cage has enough ventilation, and choosing the appropriate cage size.

3. Nutrition and Health Management: To maintain the health and vibrancy of parakeets, a

balanced food customized to meet their unique requirements is necessary. Understanding common health conditions and getting regular checkups are essential for managing and avoiding illnesses.

4. Breeding and Care: Knowing how to breed, getting ready for chicks, and giving them the care they need is essential for anybody interested in breeding. This guarantees the effective raising of young, healthy children.

Proceeding Forward

Remember that learning is an ongoing process as you go with your parakeet farming endeavors. Keep current with the most recent findings and recommended procedures in the care of birds. Participate in forums and groups dedicated to parakeet farming to exchange experiences and learn from other enthusiasts.

You should also think about establishing both short- and long-term objectives for your parakeet farm. Setting and achieving specific objectives can help you stay on track as you grow your flock, enhance care, or experiment with new breeding methods.

Last Words

The pursuit of raising parakeets is gratifying and satisfying, presenting both pleasures and difficulties. You can establish a healthy habitat for your parakeets by putting the skills and information in this book to use. Remember that commitment, lifelong learning, and a sincere love for bird care are essential for successful parakeet farming.

We are happy you could come along on this journey with us.

I hope your endeavor to raise parakeets is as colorful and happy as the birds you look after.

THE END

www.ingramcontent.com/pod-product-compliance
Lightning Source LLC
Chambersburg PA
CBHW052327220526
45472CB00001B/306